MERRIE AFRIKA!

Adam Schwartzman

Merrie Afrika!

CARCANET

First published in 1997 by
Carcanet Press Limited
4th Floor, Conavon Court
12–16 Blackfriars Street
Manchester M3 5BQ

A CIP catalogue record for this book
is available from the British Library
ISBN 1 85754 311 4

The publisher acknowledges financial assistance
from the Arts Council of England

Set in 10pt Palatino by CentraCet Ltd, Cambridge
Printed and bound in England by SRP Ltd, Exeter

Contents

Acknowledgements

Acknowledgements are due to *Slugnews* (RSA), *Quadrant* (Australia) and *PN Review, Thumbscrew, Verse, The Reader, The London Miscellany,* and the *1995 Oxford and Cambridge May Anthology,* in which versions of some of these poems first appeared. A version of IV.iv was included in the *1995 Bridport Anthology.*

'We invent for ourselves the major part of experience'
(Nietzsche, *Beyond Good and Evil*)

'"... for the rest, I ate, and drank, and slept, loved, and hated,
like another; my life was as the vapour, and is not ..."' (John
Ruskin, *Of Kings Treasuries*).

In our landscape
no aloof ships sail against the grain.
The map inscribes
no private monuments; the fine sand's
lapping at your footprints
answers
to your presence, not your name.

¶

A distant posture, a haze
of cycling feet:
as some one's millionth private mystery
moves out of view,
observe: the light that over stretch-
marked water
lights them, finds another way (especially) to you.

Part I

I.i

'Man, as the minister and interpreter of nature, can do and understand
only so much as he has observed, in fact and thought, of nature's order;
beyond this he knows nothing and can do nothing.'

(Francis Bacon, *Instauratio Magna*)

A little world, an animate clod,
a shivering rack of bones,
a web as thorough as electromagnetism,
an archipelago of souls:

with each commonplace of the schools disproved
– the divinely whirling molluscs,
the damask leaves
all in vain – the exasperated mother

of a speculative brood closes
her eyes as the children return,
the atoms of the sea
still drying out in the threads of their clothes.

The spite of stiff light
on white walls, the severe falling roses' rebuke, heat
of an infinitely orange summer
burnt out in the leaves,

the iron-hull sold or let slip
into the bay:
one sea-water flask still delicate-
ly intact, one forceps drawn to by spider's silk.

I.ii
Realworld

It was the very first Sunday when light
spread in pleats
and at ankle-height night hurried out like the shadows
cast out
under first settlers' feet.

¶

It came again the next day. It intimated
tomorrow:

a place in time for things to happen,
for evening, for morning,
for a fair working week,
for the stumbling missionary to find
fresh water,
the errant chief to be eaten by a crocodile;

and outside
a place where the rest would stay real:

for thoughts of the sullen boy
selling cassava,
the speculation of stricken daughters
– a calling place, a destination, a store house –
where plans
could wait for a National Assembly,
while date palms
grew out from where slave-traders spat.

¶

Where an open-pit sun set was Ocean,
with bits on the edges torn
back in the wind,
and fishing macorras nibbing
the distance
or numberlined safely to sea-boards.

Passion for water
was an innocent business for sailors
and poets.
Feeling for land was instinctive:
land stayed still,
you could make it seem yours,
you could build a village, keep your dead
in one place,
get your cattle to breed, plant maize-lakes and wheat,
and put dog-woods
in front of your dagga plantations.

¶

Here daylight came round
like a trick.
A sorghum plantation was where you were,
in blanket-savannah,
brachystegia woodland,
the veranda, a market, or Independence Square.
A spot of change
let you think you were stable.

The stars were more like it,
that let you doubt.

How many worried that too much was moving,
that ancestor-eyes
were too sacred to circle round you.
and midnight-lurching
on the path to the out-house
were unsettled
and half-felt the proof?

¶

Just as the traveller imagines: Gospel
from the kitchen, ease
by the inland sea, in little hands
gutting knives
a lesson in taxonomy:

the different names
of staple fish called *chambo* or *campanga*, coming easily
the first time
from children's mouths
as fathers' boats wedge in;

and unloosed from the stiff air were birds
trying out their voices all around,

¶

the grazing lands alight
with cattle
scraping their heads through the tinder-grass
as the warm morning
comes crowding in like the sudden gathering
of villagers
round stranger,

bringing tellers of stories, casters of spells,
official tasters, conductors of trade;
the promise
of a town-square, the statue
of a magistrate;
a citadel of shop-fronts. public gardens,
private properties,
stairwells tiled
with portraits, family seats and teaming backyards
to replenish and subdue.

I.iii

Some time before the proper paths
have gone up
to the peaks and the highest tea-leaves,
when the boundary-stones
are uninscribed and the ear
keeps track;
somewhere up there in those voluble hills
the singer is glistening
like an ebony curio:
every night
by the summoning-fires,
up in the hills of flint and bronze he is *on the road,*
he is *with a witness*
while skilfully the chorus is listening
to hear
if the codes of the tied-up world will appear.

I.iv
Magic

When gravity owned up to dropping the rain
the last streams
turned tail uphill, rubbing gravel back into its beds
and cowslicking cable-reeds.
Like jagged cut curtains,
thunder storms parted the sky
and the shamed sun was gaffed
in the inconstant cover
of darkness, stealing back to the east.

I.v
Merrie Africa

No one could say how, stacked up,
her horizons
slumped into each other;
even knew of the lumpy paths
beaten by hills
down to hessian shores with their limestone
interiors all simmering
like milk;

no one remembered as much as a motto
proclaimed
in a neat letter-head, or flags
and taxes being raised
in her name.

¶

Though as long as the moods
of the foremen
were brutal, and the village-thief itched like a flea
in your vest,
her silent rivers went on
whisking new bodies away through
no more than a dream,

in which sweat
in the rain was invisible,
and tears in the dark,
and grief was, as always, when nothing
else helped.

Part II

II.i

Ladies, tussling through evening colours,
double-took.
Looking up, the welder
    missed the last ring
        sliding down the blue flame

of his oxy-acetylene blade.
In the estuary the small boy
spearing flat-fish almost lost his foot.
    The lookout thought
        he'd better call the king,

who, considering the news
which he'd already got,
found his wise-man's dream
    prophesying
        encroachment from the sea had lied:

as the day went by
they saw the black marks growing clearer
in the distance were not
    headlands from another country
        but some strange kind of ship.

Secret councils were convened
as the daylight-village was displaced
in molecules and every surface
    changed its properties,
        and vague settlements marked

out the distant ladling bays at dark.
When the next day came the king
was on the shore to embrace
    his visitors, who they saw brought gifts
        and brand new opportunities.

And because he'd got it wrong
the wise-man left in shame,
whom they forgot while they were strong,
   but was later missed, and whose face
      they never saw again.

II.ii
A Civil Servant Writes Back

for Nicole Krauss

Having long since
sensed our familiar shores slipping

over the edge of the captain's log and the stars slip
a notch

on the astrolabe, we saw from the mast
a mauve cloud

turn to land,
found an unguarded bay and disembarked with a flag

– which is how I find myself here
where a grass roof burns

in fifteen minutes, a small town in half an hour;
God knows our enemies

aren't worth humbling.
Daily we wipe the scratches from our tanks.

¶

Nature, you can imagine, is a great solace to me
here: from time to time

I can almost hear roots
drawing nutrients and orchids fire up

like embers in pure air . . .
though I have also seen the hateful sun

begin to flap
off the sea, and found myself railing on against God

's filthy household,
invoking generations, age groups, a day of honour.

¶

Yet, how insufferable
our graces had grown, and the fidelity

of our old age;
how our wit left us cold

in the playhouse and our table-chat sleepy
at night;

though as for mine now,
it's still always the same: all versions of attaining

the permanent bedroom. And history too:
you might guess my desires

for return
to some broad administrative avenue or mall,

a resilient face and something in stone,
for it to be put:

here is one who drew round permanence
like a cape
and became immortally appropriate
to civilisation.

II.iii

Though the shuffling waves, approaching, fold
to the shores, and the lime sun

sets (click) like a cordial;
though palm trees claim their x deaths-

by-falling-fruit each summer,
and after warm evenings, mornings

conceive hollows
backed into the sand, before now

there was never a coastal-town here that we'd ever say
nestled in its bay.

¶

These vulnerable coasts
were where ports could fester, where sailors

sent by traders built their kiosks on the edges
of the hemisphere,

and all the tricky history came through here
on its way to happening

elsewhere, through a harbour such as this:
through onion-stone,

a garrison, a warehouse on a beach-front desperately
exfoliating in the sun;

¶

through a whirling wrought iron screen
as the harbour-master saw it

from his balcony –
the gathering in of exile, botanist, Huguenot,

prospector, crumple-robed missionary,
girl-sick soldiers

(and aching chandler's boy) –
which, retired and spitting breakfast

through his teeth, he remembers: the arch
in a broad plank

bearing weight, decent of baggage-carriers,
spray of sawdust, flying glint

of staples in the wrenching open of
an empty crate: imagine

Litvak, Isaac Schwartzman,
arrived there like a fact, imagining

the furniture he's left behind
him on a continent he'll never see again:

the polished boards, the pine
and freckled mirror glass,

the bedding set above the stove,
(whose name is balanced in the middle of mine)

¶

wandering below the Zambezi, sweating
through his linen pants,

his neck turned red,
and trading shoes and stainless steel

(his scrubland-clientele sporting free soles
on their feet)

¶

– 'til Summer finds him slung in an ox-hide
and glistening like sticky-tape:

Mashonaland.
His sight draws back; the dip and rise

of shoulders makes a sea
from the pile-thick savannah.

Matabeleland,
where the pace-singing wakes him: *Adama! Adama li-*

E-e-fa! – and the fields
would turn to yellow from green

in the laminated moon and, over the dry Limpopo, catch
in Red Seringa,

the wind ride in like drunk Cossacks:
once he saw his uncle

in his shawl, on the pavement laid out
Blessed art thou, O Lord,

and himself:
winning his way through enemies,

flames drawn back, weapons withdrawn,
and tectonic Europe,

snapping phone-lines,
come away as easily as waking up

¶

(in Cape Town) a tradesman, a lawyer, me,
two lifetimes later.

with this slow wind blowing in
from the fair, easy sea.

From here I watch the old harbour.
I imagine its traffic. I see

fishermen's children at play in the estuary.
This is my home;

this is my family; this world
is as clear as a day without meal-times

where, raised that much closer
to forms that let you see through,

we make our own proverbs: We
reign our own horses for solving problems.

(November 1994 – July 1996)

II.iv
Mombassa

The eye-thin traders, dangerous
as glass,
tearing cane in their teeth, spitting sweetly;

the crosses made of whipping-posts,
the past,
unrecoverable and safe;

under bleached white knuckles
a drudgery
of palm-trees, where the sea sold its blue skin for rain.

II.v
The East Africa Company Builds a Railway Line

All Summer
in their fenceless world the men broke stones

and smaller stones and stretcher-
bore thick sleepers

through their grazing lands: *Behold!* cried an engineer
straddling the continent

inoffensively, *our latest empire*
won with such travail . . .

¶

in the distant stock exchange
was pandemonium while,

for the first time round
with sloping wheels, the sun set, and underneath

as blinding as a teenage smile:
two great braces straightening out the ground.

II.vi

From the fort
built in the shape of a star, the lettered man,
with tape-recorder
and water-stone, rides forth
to harass the village elders
for a story.

He has come to collect some words.
He comes in peace.

Never mind his friends.

Her gentle hands throbbing with work,
the house-mother,
from her own kitchen, observes
the pith helmet's approach.
Her breasts hang over the half-door –
a pair
of ready, perfect tears.

¶

The villagers laugh
at this furrowed intent man whose chin bristles
with fire.
They laugh
at his equipment for learning,
his fragile ears catching
with zeal.

He is noting down the familiar bits,
the trail of stones, the carnivorous witch:
certainly
he has discovered in these savages
the cousin
of a known species,

while, greasing the air
with his fabulous tongue,
the town-idiot
grows yet more eloquent with attention.

II.vii
Rhodes House, Oxford

No more do you induce panic
in a crowd,
do your speech-bubbles defy perspective;

your fame is less wide-spread
than literacy,

your monogram
un-picked from a country's name.

But by your will,
you outsmarted them all, and proved
your critics wrong:

this chess-board floor and marble dome
designed to echo,

birds of prey presiding
over balustrades, and pillars right

as tooth-picks show
in no uncertain terms you lived

to be a Roman.

II.viii
Happy Valley

From the plain possession
of the family stand they stepped back

with tears in each eye and keys
in each hand,

for once they'd had parents, now no one
was evil,
       and *yea*.

in the bitterness of G
they were comforted by the easing

of T, as they walked down through valleys
bristling

with crayfish-tails of wheat.

II.ix
A Very Picture of Industry

All along the weaving streets, the sharper-
than-cicada metal *tsk tsk tsk*
was riveted in the air, and sewing machine operators,
bowed and benched,
sewed cloth,

heeling the wheels round,
with eyes so close to the pin-clip, almost necking
the shuttles and wooing the cloth
from the tables,
as the wheel neither they,

and no friend of theirs, would have thought
to inflict
reels out an unimaginable cloth – as if
history had jumped its bail
and its crumples been sewn down.

II.x
High Windows

Two light dancing-steps by the saint
appeared to be
what all the school-men were trying to express,
underneath
whose glass and lead
the mason's girl went skipping by,
sinfully unaware
of being neither still nor permanent.

Outside, the yellow sun came scouring past
but only kept the figure clean,
who made it easier
for those who stopped, to see
their landscape slightly differently.
The sinews of the air
that hold you in and mostly keep things sane
came loose around their feet.

Beyond the dislocating world the vision of the saint
was clear: inside
he taught living men first
principles, like meekness or
what, passively constructed, wood and water
properly make for,
and with their heads of cattle danced
the way to Jesus as they closed their eyes to pray.

II.xi
Ngorogoro

During which time the landscape below
stretched its forestry out,
kept the ground
to itself through the thick refractive air

and from close-up the leaves
fell down
outcrops and scarps
and rounded off contours like dustsheets.

Part III

III.i

Think of tanks rolling, a lynch mob
or stampede
and bodies touching; imagine
standing two-to-a-seat,
tight as peppercorns
in the breached VIP company boxes,

singing *Viva!*, chanting
Long Live – !,
amid banners of Union,
Guild and Youth League.
Remember us as,
not lying, the cameras showed: a sea.

III.ii
Judith Escapes with the Head of Holofernes

For all the flash of his army waking
as morning let go with its body,

her enemy,
like everything under the unshackling sun,

was as strong as its joins were hidden.
This was her new knowledge.

Unnoticed among loose-limbed corporals
and lieutenants she walks out,

a nigger with a sack the colour of wine,
leaving the tent of the Governor-

General, whose sexy death
she carries away in her hands.

¶

Just like this:
with his head in her lap, she longs

to be travelling again;
for a silent passenger over a long familiar distance,

as the landscape outside, worn thin
with effrontery,

begins shedding his names:
Livingstonia, Stanleyville, Francis Town, George;

for escape,
as the prim reverent shires of the brilliant

-ly vanquished, of long-dead brothers
and acred sons

are unseamed,
and each stone and shuffle, every turn

of phrase is homesick again
to be something.

¶

Now she sees in perspectives
only, the line between backdrop and rise

reveal the journey,
the winding route straighten out;

and they go through
by the necessary passes and drives.

III.iii
Tiwi

During which time the wind threw our voices
that levelled
a cloud-bank, and rattled
through half-fastened windows
like a walkman treble,

and lengths of thatch
popped beads off their ends and shot dotted lines
and, their clothes stuck
to familiar shapes, suddenly
even the beautiful were living short lives.

III.iv

Looking out on some *rue*
with its extraneous history going on
in its own fashion entirely,
he was a thousand miles away
attending to letters in a foreign café
almost ready to believe it all,
not least – he found – the bits that seemed
most true.

Far from the roar
and hill of applause, the waiting
for a sudden circumstance
to seem like providence or revelation,
he longed to be crawling
through foliage to the border,
his principle concern the safety of the journalist,
the rolls of film and the story.

Whoever'd sat there last left roses
in a half-filled glass, which dropped pages
from its supple spine and wept
encyclopaedias of scent
on the chequered cloth: thus he dealt with the state
at least of some one's affairs
and passed his days in illustrious company:
Tiresius, Danté, the young Haile Selassie.

So when in the end he attained
for a pension his exile's return, he chose
a time not terribly hungry at words,
where, in the scribbled yards
the gas canisters purred,
and soon enough came the silk rains
easing out from the svelte wet air.
Unexplosively, it was going to be another day.

III.v

Like bathers
walking into a plane, or vast distances

squashed by perspective;

as if pulled away
to some centrifugal Rome.

Death wows us in its usual way.
Such love exceeds us. Another celebration!

III.vi

In some places the earth is flat – wind
and gradient bring
everything together: voices drift out
from across the plane –
hours later the bodies.

Getting no closer nor farther away,
the sun comes
right down; surrounded by one straight line
we know: never stay
too long in one place, or be counted
in a doorway.

Something no one sees is all around:
trees melt
into ant-hills; yeast-clouds bloom above a
length of gauze.
Under the hot sun we live
at the mercy of each other.

III.vii
Retrospect

i

Scraping light from a match,
turning easily on a step we remember
an altogether different place.

The sky was white with rain.
In the cemeteries the marble wept.
How late it was.

Some one invisible knew
your address;
some one your route to the café by heart.

Rain falls and reaches pavements.
In the city it rains
and fridges sigh and drops trace faces

we remember
in wrought iron mazes, gathering
on balustrades.

ii

When it's easy to turn
in an ampler light we remember
an altogether different place

where the wet ground
kept track, and the streams found out our paths.
How late it was:

hearing the engine, being almost at the gate,
big events happening like a lead slap
on the back of the neck.

Rain falls and reaches pavements.
The weather-man smiles
in black and white and we look back:

we remember
the short winds jolting through the city streets,
and the grubby intricacies of state intrigue.

iii

Desiring a match
(as the light turns so easily) we remember
an altogether different place

where crinkle-brush caught the wind, and dust
zipped up the trees.
How late it was.

In the houses of lawyers the telephones ring.
A vigil is kept.
You were, as the editor writes, quite exemplary.

Rain falls and reaches pavements
and as hesitant water expands
into space

we imagine
in an altogether different way
those who deserved to be alive today.

Part IV

IV.i
Ride

The ruts snapped at my tyres. The wind
pinned back sound
over the walkways and ridgeway girders.

Through a shower of blossoms
I was riding my bicycle: understand, my love,
that we had
for a moment quite attained,

that the trees waved their flags; how everyone,
for a time, was a President.

IV.ii
Troia Nova

Most unbelievably,
the creased, encumbered, white-bellied sky,
the land-intending swans,
stiff-necked, gathering air;

and lesser signs:
the banks of neon's swell and ebb
like grain,
and pavements embroidered with tea-leaves.

¶

After a perilous journey, each last-minute sacrifice,
a Capital
rising round its landmarks:
Radio Station

(treasury of words)
guarded like a wallet, Legislature and Court
held tight
as private parts;

the spectacular frescoes of iron
and plastic,
cooking pots and nasturtiums, rubies
aglow among fuscias,

the intimate secrets
of street signs inscribed
in each corner
like billet-doux, in the city, *boudoir* of the repossessed.

IV.iii
Backpacker

Appearing among a flotilla
of teeth
in a windy bay, a straw hat lost
to the breeze, time
   over the aluminium-paved sea,
     (breakfast behind the customs-stalls)

the tireless seeker of hinterlands
arrives, preferrer
of stars in the sky, the wind
in his corner,
   blond wisps in his nape,
     white cotton on a tanned throat.

Enter the soon-to-be honourably dirty,
to quest for themselves
in a difficult place:
from the first turning back
   in the foothills
     to entropy-hike on approach to the roadblock.

Shunners of the home-from-home emporium,
sleeping tonight in an unlit city,
they fear the devil,
the button-riddled waiters,
   crimson order
     of the wide-bladed gash,

though even pursued over plains
by the dust,
they are met by nothing
so serious as absence: the pleasantly refracted
   faces they find
     in the pools are their own: the planter's of tea,

the reader's of fine-printed fortunes
in alluvial pans.
Now common as anthracite,

they are malleably warm in memory's palm:
    worth a trip to the island,
        or a knife on the beach from the artless.

So may their patron saints
protect them
from officials and malaria; may their currency
not debase;   .
    among crimpeline stalactites and exorbitant massifs
      may they remain

consistently endogenous, who know
that without them the flowers will rust, the windmills
turn eternally,
that, with each day so quick
    to recover
      at last it will be yesterday again.

IV.iv

Under the blue-printed sky or in hotel rooms
the smart young aides slept,
who were none the poorer
when the crinkled rills began turning back
up the creeks,
and the wavy streams repaired to the hills:
for a time the air was still
a nice colour for a shirt,
the flowers still crazy with light.

Their leaving was nothing more
than a hair lifting, than the turning of the wind,
a brushing against a cheek,
though eventually everyone
began dreaming of rain, became haunted
by the ammonia smell
of the long-overdue afternoon squalls
whipping by in profile,
and sooner or later, rocked

in the *primum mobile* of their huddled sleep,
it would be them
in the city-bound carriages, imagining
the sound of the train
become the sound of storms,
while up the sun drove
in perennial white and, slowly,
the land lost its memory for knowing
who, where, why, how many, how many times before.

IV.v
Massacre

The peddler takes another route
from the one he took before,
lifting thin grass,
resurrecting an old path with a horse.

The conspiratorial tones
of Naturalists breathing through the leaves
make known
an absolutely usual landscape:

the mundane overhead flapping of summer flocks,
the harmless folds
of rivers gently tearing their banks,
bark buckling

in the lazy trees like sedimentary rock.

IV.vi
Tanga

During which time
to easily move and to eat

is enough;
and to walk on the red and black marble of the low tide beach,

the mirror flats, the crumpled tissue sea;
observe

port-side acacias from the portico, swoop
into the evening,

as all the world becomes different
shades

of the same colour, and ourselves so comfortable,
and right and free.

IV.vii
Erosion

Through gullies draped with canvas pleats
the weather cut
– avenging angel, archaeologist divine –
stripping earth
of artefact and hydroscopic loyalty.

To cede the tillage of this region or
that plain,
the ancient dead were dusted off
and lost the map
more surely than a civil war.

Overhead the birds looked on a screwed up face,
a sandstone frieze,
a crumpled ball, an ancient scroll,
a landscape cleared
for God's next most chosen race.

IV.viii
Dar Es Salaam

During which time, blacking out, the sky spits
a cob-full of molars,

shakes and blusters with light, and shaking
off blankets or whores

the uncoffeed
descend each old white-washed splinter-wood floor

through the gossip and hum in the air,
in whose space

belongs the sounds of everyone:
he, the enterer, she

the forlorn, you, the strictly unperturbed, me,
the freshly undone.

IV.ix
Lines for a Plaque in Harry's Hotel, Nyahururu

Let the unsure lichen be vindicated
that never grew here,

and in clean stone see
how another group passing through got on:

more or less uneasily.

IV.x
Brochure

Pixels of light
at 6 a.m. fire off the cathode lake,

making a fuzz;
the first birds begin slapping into the sky

like screaming girls;
others, struggling to find gear, ratchet

through the air;
frogs start up like motorbikes; palms rattle:

a most suitable landscape
is scrolling by.

Hippos rise like scupppered barges at low tide,
evacuating their hulls;

down the valves of their nostrils
buffaloes breathe;

while further off a leopard roars like a Leyland
changing down,

then accelerating
into a day as at home

as anywhere
here in the twentieth century.

During which time
cling-wrapped flamingos shimmied
on water
and marabous tap-danced on tree tops,

and pelican islands
dissolved
into soda and streamers manoeuvred
in a white liquid sky;

¶

in a white liquid sky
                    (as white
as an iris
aspiring to sculpture),

the chafing spectrum flashed to its outlines,

and one summer
was the mnemonics of a landscape, and
the light whooping
out from some anonymous scrubland.

Notes

I've noted below bits and pieces in the poems that are adaptations, incorporations, quotations, translations, are in need of translation into English, or are engaging with certain sets of ideas in certain ways that may not be familiar to any one of the many communities out of which the poems are written. Needless to say, these annotations are not a commentary, nor do they provide a rationale for the poems.

I.i   Donne, for instance, writes in his *Divine Meditations*: 'I am a little world made cunningly/Of elements, and an angelic sprite...' – a standard Renaissance description of man's place in the universe. The version I used for my poem I came across in Walter Pater's essay on Pico Della Mirandola, in which he translates from the 'Second Proem' of Pico's *Heptaplus*:

> It is a commonplace of the schools that man is a little world, in which we may discern a body mingled of earthly elements, and ethereal breath, and the vegetable life of plants, and the senses of the lower animals, and reason, and the intelligence of the angels, and a likeness to God.

I.ii   This poem is a *gecyndboc*, a book of origin. I closely followed Dr J. H. Hertz's 1938 dual text edition of the Pentateuch in drawing on *Bereshith*, Chapter 1.
macorra: a canoe, made from a hollowed out tree trunk.
dagga: cannabis

I.iii   '*on the road*' and '*with a witness*' are paraphrases of parts of the audience response in the transcription of an Afro-American sermon I came accross in Viv Edwards's and Thomas J. Sienkewicz's *Oral Cultures Past and Present* (1991), p. 88.

II.iii   The poem was suggested by the extraordinarily cool description by John Saccarrol of the landing of the Earl of Cumberland's fleet in Sierra Leone in 1586, quoted in the fifth chapter of Stephen Greenblatt's *Renaissance Self-Fashioning*:

The fourth of November we went on shore to a town of the Negroes ... which we found to be but lately built: it was of about two hundred houses, and walled about with mighty great trees, and stakes so thick, that a rat could hardly get in or out. But as it chanced, we came directly upon a port which was not shut up, where we entered with such fierceness, that the people fled all out of the town, which we found to be finely built after their fashion, and the streets of it so intricate that it was difficult for us to find the way out that we came in at. We found their houses and streets so finely and cleanly kept that it was an admiration to us all, for that neither in the houses nor streets was so much dust to be found as would fill an egg shell. We found little in their houses, except some mats, gourds, and some earthen pots. Our men at their departure set the town on fire, and it was burnt (for the most part of it) in a quarter of an hour, the houses being covered with reed and straw.

II.iii 'Litvak': Yiddish term for a Jew originally from Lithuania.

'Adama! Adama li-/E-e-fa': The first phrase of a hymn – literally 'Adam and Eve' – transcribed as you hear it sound off the tongue.

II.iv The cross made of a whipping post is actually in the Old Slave Market, Stone Town, Zanzibar.

II.v 'fenceless world': cf. Milton's description of the 'first grand Thief', *Paradise Lost*, Book IV, ll. 171–192

'Behold! ... our latest empire won with such travail': cf. Book: X, ll. 591–595.

II.viii Happy Valley was the name given to a fertile area in Kenya's 'White Highlands', occupied by settlers renowned for an exorbitant ex-patriot lifestyle.

'From the plain possession': cf. *II Henry IV*, IV.v, ll. 221–222: 'You won it, wore it, kept it, gave it me;/ Then plain must my possession be.'

'yea, in the bitterness ...': cf. Psalm 23.

III.vi Although events like those alluded to in this poem were repeated a thousand times in countless operations which South Africa's Truth and Reconciliation Commission began uncovering in 1996, in writing this poem I had in mind specifically the assassinations of South African Communist Party Leader, Chris Hani, and political activist and lawyer, Griffiths Mxenge.

IV.i *'Troia Nova'*: Literally 'New Troy' which, in Geoffrey of Monmouth's *History of the Kings of Britain*, is the name given to London by its legendary founder, Brutus.

The poem draws on a number of images from *The Aeneid*, baring on the movement from old to new Troy. I used David West's prose translation, Penguin Classics (1991).

'the creased, encumbered, white-bellied sky': cf. Book III, ll. 389–393:

> When in an hour of perplexity by the flowing waters of a lonely river you find under some holm-oaks on the shore a great sow with the litter of thirty piglets she has farrowed, lying there on her side all white, with her young all white around her udders, that will be the place for your city.

'land intending swans . . .': cf. Book I, ll. 393–400:

> Look at these twelve swans flying joyfully in formation. The eagle of Jupiter was swooping down on them from the heights of heaven and scattering them over the open sky, but now look at them in their long column. Some are reaching land. Some have already reached it and are looking down on it. Just as they have come to their home and their flock has circled the sky in play, singing as they fly with whirring wings, so your ships and your warriors are crossing the bar in full sail.

'banks of neon . . .': cf. Book II, ll. 302–305:

> I shook the sleep from me and climbed to the highest gable of the roof, and stood there with my ears pricked up like a shepherd when a furious south wind is carrying fire into a field of grain . . .

'pavements embroidered with tea-leaves': cf. Book III, 445–452:

> After she [the Sibyl] has written her prophecies on these leaves she seals them all up in her cave where they stay in their appointed order. But the leaves are so light that when the door turns in its sockets the slightest breath of

wind dislodges them. The draught from the door throws them into confusion and the priestess never makes it her concern to catch them as they flutter round her rocky cave and put them back in order or join up the prophecies.

IV.iv Lloyd Timberlake's provocative *Famine in Africa* (1987) provided the initial impetus, and some of the background, for the writing of this poem.

Epilogue Pater discusses the idea of *Algemeinheid* – that is, breadth, generosity, universality – in his essay on Winckleman:

> [Sculpture] has had, indeed, from the beginning an unfixed claim to colour; but this element of colour in its has always been more or less conventional, with no melting or modulations of tones, never permitting more than a very limited realism. It was maintained chiefly as a religious tradition. In proportion as the art of sculpture ceased to be merely decorative, and subornative to architecture, it threw itself upon pure form. It renounces the power of expression by lower or heightened tones. In it, no member of the human form is more significant that the rest; the eye is wide, and without pupil; the lips and brow are hardly less significant than hands, and breasts and feet. But the limitation of its resources is part of its pride: it has no background, no sky or atmosphere, to suggest and interpret a train of feeling; a little of suggested motion, and much of pure light on its gleaming surfaces, with pure form – only these. And it gains more by this limitation to its own distinguishing motives: its unveils man in the repose of his unchanging characteristics. That white light, purged from the angry, bloodlike stains of action and passion, reveals, not what is accidental in man, but the tranquil godship in him, as opposed to the restless accidents of life.